NORTHUMBERLAND
SCHOOLS LIBRARY SERVICE

This book should be returned on or before the last date stamped
below unless an extension of the loan period is granted.
Application for renewal may be made by letter or telephone.

IN THE PAST

Popcorn

House and Home

Dereen Taylor

WAYLAND

Explore the world with **Popcorn** - your complete first non-fiction library.

Look out for more titles in the **Popcorn** range. All books have the same format of simple text and striking images. Text is carefully matched to the pictures to help readers to identify and understand key vocabulary.
www.waylandbooks.co.uk/popcorn

First published in 2009 by Wayland

Copyright © Wayland 2009

Wayland
Hachette Children's Books
338 Euston Road
London NW1 3BH

Wayland Australia
Level 17/207 Kent Street
Sydney NSW 2000

Editor: Julia Adams
Designer: Alix Wood
Picture researcher: Diana Morris

British Library Cataloguing in Publication Data:
Taylor, Dereen
    House and home. - (Popcorn. In the past)
    1. Dwellings - History - Juvenile literature 2. Housing -
    History - Juvenile literature
    I. Title
    392.3'6'09
    ISBN 978 0 7502 5779 4

Printed and bound in China

Wayland is a division of Hachette Children's Books,
an Hachette UK Company.
www.hachette.co.uk

Acknowledgements:
Alfieri/Topfoto: 4. Classic
Stock/Topfoto: 20. Mary Evans PL:
17. fine art/Alamy: 15. Owen
Franken/Corbis: 21. Hemis/Corbis:
5. Hulton Deutsch Collection/
Corbis: front cover,1, 6, 10, 14, 19.
Jewish Chronicle/HIP/Topfoto: 2,
12. Picturepoint/Topfoto: 8, 11, 13,
16. Howard Sochurek/Time
Life/Getty Images: 9. Topfoto: 7.
Topical Press/Hulton Archive/Getty
Images: 18.
Andy Crawford: 23.

Contents

Different houses

A hundred years ago, many families lived in cramped terraced houses. Some even shared these houses with other families.

Children often played out in the streets because their homes had no gardens.

1920s

Rich families lived in detached houses. The houses were so big, there were even rooms for servants to live in.

The family who lived in this Victorian house probably had many servants to look after them.

Building houses

In Victorian times, builders did not have any machines, like cranes. This is why many buildings were not more than two storeys high.

These builders are using wheelbarrows to move bricks and heavy material.

1865

After World War II, builders used many machines, so they were able to build much higher buildings.

1964

This block of flats in London is 20 storeys high. Can you see all the machines that are being used to build it?

Water and electricity

Until the 1940s, it was not common for houses to have taps with running water. Families used water from a pump outside.

1933

Poor families often shared a water pump between them.

There was no electric lighting
in many homes until the 1930s.
People used oil lamps instead.

The light from oil lamps was very dim.
People needed many lamps to light up a room.

Heating

Most homes did not have central heating until the 1960s. Rooms had open fireplaces instead.

Families sat around the fire together because the rest of the house was so cold.

1946

People sometimes used paraffin heaters. Paraffin smelt horrible and made the walls damp.

1949

These children are trying to keep warm. Can you see the paraffin heater?

Upstairs

In poor families, children shared bedrooms with their brothers and sisters. They often shared beds too, because there was no heating.

1965

Rich families sometimes had a special room upstairs for children to play in. This was called a nursery.

1933

What are the children playing with in this nursery?

Bathroom

Many homes did not have bathrooms
until the 1930s. Baths were taken in
a tin bath in the living room.

In the summer, families sometimes had
their bath in the garden.

1910

Poor families lived in houses that had outside toilets. Some houses still had them until the 1970s.

1972

This toilet has a chain to pull to flush it.

Until the 1950s, many people used squares of newspaper for toilet paper!

Kitchen

In the past, kitchens had a range. One side was a boiler that heated water. The other was an oven for cooking and baking.

1936

This housewife has baked Cornish pasties in the range.

Households did not have fridges or freezers before the 1950s. Food was stored on shelves in a pantry.

Meat was hung on hooks in pantries to keep it fresh.

Washing

Before there were washing machines, washing clothes was hard work. The clothes had to be scrubbed by hand.

1939

Washing machines became more common in the 1950s and 1960s.

Clothes were scrubbed on a washboard to clean them.

When the washing was clean, it was squeezed to get most of the water out.

Wet clothes were hung up over the range to dry.

1940s

Home comforts

New inventions, like vacuum cleaners and washing machines, made housework much quicker and easier to do.

1950s

Before the 1970s, most families used carpet sweepers to keep their carpets clean.

By the 1970s, many homes were warmer, more comfortable places to live.

1975

The first televisions showed only black and white programmes.

Timeline

1860s Paraffin lamps are introduced.

1900s Many terraced houses are built until the 1900s.
Most homes have no running water or inside toilets.

1940s Few homes have fitted carpets, televisions or telephones.

1948 A quarter of British homes still have no electricity.

1950s Many new houses are built using cranes and machines.
Fridges and washing machines are more common
in households.

1960s Many terraced houses still have outside toilets.
Most homes have central heating.

1963 Introduction of the first upright vacuum cleaner,
like the ones used today.

1970s Most homes have a television set.

1990s The first DVD players arrive in British homes.

Design a house

Make your own Victorian house plan.

First, decide what sort of house you are going to draw a plan for. It could be a large detached house or small terrace, with an outside toilet and a water pump in the yard.

1. Use a ruler to draw the rooms and the staircase of your house.
This is the downstairs part.

2. If your house has a toilet and a water pump outside, leave room on the side of the paper for them.

3. Draw lines to show where the doors are. Use a bold colour to label each room.

4. Use coloured pens to draw the furniture. Use the other sheet of paper to design the upstairs part of your house.

Glossary

central heating   A system that heats buildings through a boiler and radiators in each room.

detached house   A house that is not joined to another house.

pantry   A cupboard or small room for storing food.

pasty   A pastry filled with meat and vegetables.

range   An oven heated by wood or coal.

terraced house   A house joined to another house on both sides.

Victorian   Belonging to the time when Queen Victoria was on the throne (1837–1901).

washboard   A wooden or metal board with ridges used to scrub wet clothes clean.

Index